ECHOES
OF
MY SHADOW
—— CHILDHOOD

ROBIN GINTHER VENNERI

Print ISBN 979-8-9875591-1-6

First edition, 2023
KIPS Publishing

Expose yourself to your deepest fear, whatever that may
be.
After that, fear has no power, control, or foundation; only
then are you truly free!

"Love yourself because no amount of love from others is
sufficient to fill the longing that your soul requires from
you."

And with that,

**Let's not just slay our demons;
let's dissect them and find out what's been
feeding them!**

SHADOW SELF

Everyone carries a "shadow self" within - the part of us that contains our deepest fears and shame yet is so often hidden away from society. We all have one, but if we ignore it instead of embracing it as an integral part of ourselves, those repressed parts can manifest in negative ways later in life. Doing shadow work means taking the time to discover this hidden side and make peace with who you really are!

So, what's your shadow self hiding?

Unlocking and understanding your shadow self can be a difficult journey. It requires courage to look deep within yourself, come face-to-face with past trauma or negative beliefs you may have picked up along the way, and revel in the imperfections of those around you--including yourself! While it takes work to process these emotions that make us uncomfortable at times, this courageous undertaking grants access to powerful growth potential—allowing for more meaningful relationships and greater mental clarity. In other words? An invitation toward transformation awaits when we bravely open our minds (and hearts) on the quest to discover our true selves.

I have been in this "phase" probably most of my life, where I can't talk about it because if I do, it matters. If it matters. That means it's real, and if it's real, it will hurt.

Today though, I am in the "phase" of sometimes you need to talk about something, not to get sympathy or help but to kill the power they have over you by admitting the truth. So today, I say with quivering breath: I'm a survivor of molestation and rape. And yeah, it's making me puke to say it out loud.

It's been three weeks since I last worked on this part of the book. I ran away from my feelings and emotions. I wanted to hide; I did everything but finish this paragraph. I cleaned, organized, cried, ate nonstop, and did so many destructive and evasive behaviors that I'm now telling you not to do. I get it. It hurts; it fucking hurts.

Ok, I am back now. I am not here to point fingers, enact revenge or even get sympathy but to heal myself.

I'm 53 years old, and it's about damn time that I live without this shadow hanging over me 24/7 and move on with my life.

With that said, here's a quote that really resonates with me: "Your trauma made you stronger."

"No, my trauma traumatized me; it made me weak, gave me sleepless nights and memory loss, and gave me feelings I've never wanted. So I made myself stronger by dragging myself out of a dark place and dealing with consequences that weren't my fault."

BENEFITS OF SHADOW WORK

Why should I put myself through this?

Because

Shadow work may release energy
Your shadow twin has long-forgotten skills and talents
Meeting your shadow gives you power
You're more likely to project onto others positively
You're less likely to project onto others negatively
Shadow work frees you from limitations!
Shadow work helps you to feel whole
Shadow work enables feeling at ease in the present
Shadow Work can help with your physical well-being
Shadow work improves your close relationships
Friendships can improve with shadow work
Shadow work may quiet the racing thoughts
Shadow work may help you to stop repeating patterns
Shadow work helps to heal ancestral traumas
Shadow work enables understanding of family trauma
Working with your shadow twin is to perceive yourself as timeless.
Shadow work enables you to release fear
Shame can be released through shadow work
Help heal your piece of the feminine or masculine shadow

VOICES OF THE SELF

THE MIND:

Endless chatter or racing thoughts that fills up space

INNER CHILD:

Looking for validation and protection or even attention

THE EGO:

Constantly looking to prove itself

THE SOUL:

A quiet clarity that sometimes goes unnoticed

SO WHO ARE YOU LISTENING TO?

EMOTIONAL SELF-CARE

SET HEALTHY BOUNDARIES

Healthy boundaries will determine the acceptable behavior of others around you and how you will react when someone attempts to cross those limitations.

LEARN TO SAY NO

It will give you a sense of empowerment while actively helping you preserve your relationships.

ACCEPT

The key to dealing with negative events is to accept them as they are. It will save you a great deal of time and trouble.

ALLOW YOURSELF TO LET GO

Simply allow yourself to let go of things that no longer serve you. Otherwise, it will hinder your growth.

SELF-FORGIVENESS

Self-forgiveness is essential for moving ahead in life in a healthier way.

WHAT IS SELF-SOOTHING?

Adults can learn how to self-soothe and deal with their stress in order to help them develop healthy, positive habits. Through consistent practice of calming techniques during times of stress or anxiety, adults will eventually be able to naturally do these things without having to think about them consciously. Establishing good routines incorporating self-care activities is an excellent way for adults to increase their ability to manage life's pressures!

Transform your reactions to negative situations with the power of positive self-talk. With intentional practice, you can create a new normal where kindness and gentleness replace feelings of doubt or insecurity. Put these comforting words into action: "Even though this feels tough right now, I know I'm strong enough to work through it." Keep going - soon enough, Self Love will become second nature!

Spending time in nature, such as walking in the woods, can be a great way to reduce stress and gain composure—it creates an environment of visual calmness away from the hustle and bustle of everyday life. You can take many other approaches to combat stress and look inward. Distracting yourself from your favorite movie or TV show provides a welcome distraction; drawing or coloring pictures, adjusting lighting and smells, reading books, and listening to music are all enjoyable ways to escape from reality. It is important to find what tactics work for you and use them when needed. Invest time in activities devoted to self-care, as this will have long-term mental health benefits. Take advantage of these moments for restorative peace so that not only can you deal better with stress but also bring back joy into your life once again!

As you can see, there are a variety of ways to create an environment of relaxation, which will, in turn, reduce anxiety. From noise machines and aromatherapy to having a taste distraction or baking your favorite treat, these actions can distract from racing thoughts and make sleeping easier at night. Being conscious of the tools that can help with nighttime stress is important and will not only lead to fewer sleepless nights but also provide peace of mind. It's never easy dealing with racing thoughts late at night or not falling asleep easily, but it doesn't have to be impossible, either. Take time for yourself every day by doing something calming or enjoyable and put yourself into a relaxed state before bedtime; achieving inner peace will be easier than you feared!

While the idea of changing clothes might sound like a small act, it can make a huge difference in how you choose to handle your negative feelings. When we allow ourselves to observe the distress without trying to fight against it, we are making progress toward being in control and, therefore, more at peace. Remember this quote: "Uncontrolled emotions cannot be tamed - they can only be channeled" - Ben Lerner. Our emotions do not unbind us; instead, we can take actions that better equip us to navigate them. If you're feeling overwhelmed or anxious, take the time to reflect on what YOU can do or change, then start small and build from there, from engaging in mindfulness exercises such as mindful walking or counting your breaths to putting on those comfy PJs just for fun. Whatever the case may be for you, the key is self-care and self-love because when we pay attention and show up for ourselves, so many good things can happen too!

Instead of fighting negative thoughts, acknowledge them. Don't try to "right" or "wrong" them; just let them be. Sometimes if you fixate on negative emotions, you'll start to feel "anxieties ABOUT your anxieties"! Be kind to yourself.

Always remember, You Do You, Boo!

THINK INSIDE THE BOX

Vision Board

A vision board aims to manifest a mood, goal, or idea. Either digitally or physically, This will help shift your mindset.

Manifestation Box

Also known as an intention box, vision box, or wish box, it manifests a certain mood, goal, or idea in physical box form. This, too, will help shift your mindset using the law of attraction.

A manifestation, vision, law of attraction, creation, wish, and intention box can be a powerful tool in creating the life you want! The idea is to place things in the box you want to attract or manifest in your life. Then, you send an affirmation to the universe each time you do, and your intentions will begin to draw your desires.

Self Soothing Box

A self-soothe box is a box you make that contains things that ground you, make you feel more relaxed, and reduce symptoms of panic, anxiety, emotional distress, or low mood.

VISION BOARD

So, how do we create a powerful vision board to manifest our desires?

STEP 1: SET YOUR VISION

The first step of creating any vision board is, of course, to set your vision. Then, take some time to think about what you want to manifest in your life.

With your intention in mind, spend some time thinking about how you'd ***feel*** if you had your desire right now.

These are all things you want to portray in your vision board, which will make your board such a powerful tool for you!

STEP 2: CHOOSE YOUR FORMAT

Now that you have a solid vision, it's time to figure out how to create a digital or physical vision board.

STEP 3: GATHER YOUR IMAGES

The idea is to take images that connect you to your vision. If a picture helps you visualize your end goal, it's the perfect candidate for your board!

STEP 4: CREATE YOUR BOARD

Now that you have your image collection, it's time to create a board representing your vision to add them to your platform of choice.

Make sure to add inspiring words, too, as these can help when using your board for manifestation!

STEP 5: PUT YOUR VISION BOARD EVERYWHERE

You can print and frame it in your room like you might with a physical board or add it to your bookmarks or favorites on every device, so it's easily accessible whenever you need it.

Or better yet, add your board to your home screen and lock screens, so it's always in sight when using your digital devices!

There is no right or wrong way to do this.

MANIFESTATION BOX

So, how do we create a powerful manifestation, wish, intention, law of attraction, or Feng Shui silver box to manifest our desires?

Step 1: Find or make a small box with a lid. Get creative and decorate your box to your liking.

Step 2: Cut small strips of paper – big enough to write down your wishes.

Step 3: Write each wish on a single slip of paper and put it in the box.

Start each wish with: I wish…(and complete it with your desire or hope for something to happen). Example: I want to visit Italy.

Step 4: Write as many wishes as you like. BELIEVE in your heart that what you wish for will come true.

Step 5: Put your Wish Box in a special place.

Step 6: On occasion, you'll be able to look through your wishes. Remove the wishes that have come true and those that no longer matter to you. You can always add new ones.

SELF-SOOTHE BOX

Struggling to stay rooted in the present moment? A self-soothe box might be your saving grace! They offer a variety of sensory distractions that help keep emotions under control and provide comforting relief. When you're feeling zen, craft one together with items from all five senses: vision (flashcards), smell (essential oils or lotions), sound(relaxing music?), taste, and touch -- get creative & pick things that make you feel calm. Your personalized well-being kit is just moments away! Here are a few suggestions:

VISION

Take a break from the world and cherish precious memories with your personalized Self-Soothe Box. Fill it up with photos of your family and snapshots of calming landscapes, or get creative by adding postcards! Coloring books are also great for self-soothing as they help lower stress levels while enhancing concentration - so consider having those in there, alongside some coloring pencils!

SMELL

Our sense of smell has powerful associations with memories, making it a potent tool in self-soothing. Create your calming oasis by utilizing scents like essential oils, candles, or diffusers to bring back positive moments and reduce stress levels.

SOUND

Reach for a little peace of mind with your self-soothe box. Explore different ways to relax, from chilling out to some music or podcasts through nature sounds that draw you closer to the moment--it all depends on what works best for YOU! Why not keep white noise nearby as an easy option when life gets tough? Create an upbeat playlist and embrace it during hard times; happy vibes can help calm those frazzled nerves.

TASTE

For those moments when life gets too chaotic, you can find some relaxation with the right snacks. Mints and chocolate provide calming sweetness, while sour treats give a zing of energy to center your focus. Tea lovers won't be disappointed either; herbal varieties make for great anxiolytics in addition to being delicious drinks! And don't forget about water: keeping hydrated isn't just healthy—it also helps maintain even breathing during a stressful situation or panic attack.

TOUCH

Feeling overwhelmed? Strengthening your body to relax and counteract stress can be as easy as finding something you can squeeze or hold. Get creative with it – therapy putty, spiky balls, fluffy fabric, feathers, and even a hand cream are all great options for releasing tension that manifests in our bodies when we're feeling especially strained. Try out these tactile tools & let the calming vibes flow!

3M's

Mindfulness Meditation in five Minutes
Take three deep breaths.

You'll notice thoughts racing across your brain as you sit there.
Acknowledge them, but try not to fixate on them.

Accept all the noises you hear around you. They aren't distractions; they're simply the natural rhythm of your current space. All you need to do right now is sit and breathe.

Your mind is probably jumping from thought to thought.
This is normal. Don't worry about your racing mind; focus on your body's breath going in and out.

Observe the energy of your breath. When a thought pops into your head, release it and focus on your breathing.

Follow the breath in and follow the breath out. Let go of expectations about how this meditation will go, and keep bringing your focus back to your breath.

Feel your diaphragm rise and retreat with each passing breath.

And just like that, you have meditated.

ABCs of Mindfulness

AWARENESS Ask yourself, "is it true

BREATHING "Breathe and let the thought pass through without judging it."

COMPASSION "Counter it with a positive thought."

MEDITATE

Meditating after your shadow work helps to balance things out. I'm not really into meditation, not how it is portrayed on social media.

You know, when you are on the treadmill, and your mind goes off on its own, yup, that's mediation, or when you're in the grocery store bobbing and weaving doing your shopping, and your mind wanders, yup, that's mediation. Or when you hear a favorite song and turn it up and dance to it, that's mediation or a form of it. It is a loose form of moving meditation, and you know what? It's a fine start. And if later you pick up yoga or guided or focused meditation, all the better. But It does help clear your mind, ground you, and settle your racing thoughts. At least, it did for me.

Practicing self-care afterward does two things:

It comforts you and makes you feel better after an uncomfortable shadow work session. It helIn addition, it helps you form a positive association with your shadow work practice. If I do this, I will get a bubble bath, cupcake, or a glass of wine.

And self-care is like giving yourself a mental and physical emotional bear hug.

Write about other stuff in your journal too.
When I journal, I start with whatever I have done during the day. I then move on to food and what I ate, and then I get down to business.

Try starting with gratitude, setting goals/intentions, scheduling self-care activities, and writing affirmations. Whatever you feel comfortable with at the time.

Next, you can have a friend "hold space" (see my definition) for you while talking about your discoveries, but you don't have to. You could seek counseling if you don't want a friend to know. Either way can be cathartic, but You Do You! But remember, shadow work brings buried emotions and shadow traits to the surface so that we can heal and deal with them. This way, we can move on and grow.

Shadow work takes time and practice. So you need to learn how to deal with negative emotions healthily before you dig up a load of shit that will make you feel awful and prevent you from doing any more Shadow work ever again.

Here we go,
I have added some templates that you might find helpful. But It's up to which ones you want to use.

GET SHIT DONE

CATCH
WHAT NEEDS LOOKED AT?

1. ______________________________

____

2. ______________________________

____

3. ______________________________

____

____

____

____

____

HAPPY THOUGHTS

1. ______________________________

____

2. ______________________________

____

3. ______________________________

VOMIT BUCKET
GET RID OF THAT SHIT!

____

____

____

____

____

____

____

____

____

____

____

____

____

RELEASE
WHAT NEEDS LET GO?

1. ______________________________

____

2. ______________________________

____

3. ______________________________

____

GOAL: ______________________________

MY MIND

WHAT'S ON MY MIND RIGHT NOW?
WHAT IS HOLDING ME BACK?

AREAS I NEED CLARITY IN

THINGS I CAN DO TO CHILL

MENTAL STRUGGLES

THINGS THAT'VE BEEN BOTHERING ME LATELY

THINGS THAT ARE FRUSTRATING ME THAT I CAN VOMIT AWAY?

HOLDING SPACE?

This is from the other books that I found to be helpful.

"Holding space" means being physically, mentally, and emotionally present for someone. It means focusing on someone to support them as they work through their feelings. An essential aspect of holding space is managing judgment while you are present.

How do you tell someone you are holding space for them?
Let them know you are there to solely listen and provide a space for them to express themselves if they want to. But, on the other hand, please don't assume someone wants to talk about their feelings, and reassure them that you believe them.
Remind them that you trust and believe in their knowledge and intuition. Holding space, it's like creating a metaphorical bucket for someone to emotionally and verbally vomit into. That sounds nasty, but it's true.

So, if you are too tired to speak, sit next to me because I, too, am fluent in silence.
~R. Arnold

HOW TO HOLD SPACE

Here are the things you need to bring to support someone and what they need to bring to support you:

Creating a supportive space for another can be accomplished through loving-kindness, deep listening, and unconditional positive regard. Sitting with someone without interruption is also an important part of this process; simply being present shows that you care. By employing these techniques, it is possible to support others while cultivating meaningful connections based on trust and understanding - something many desperately seek out in today's world!

Listening and understanding without judgment are what holding space for someone looks like. Taking a non-reactive approach -- not trying to change anything, just allowing them to express their feelings -- creates an environment of safety and trust. When the urge arises to do something, instead take some time for your breath; it will keep you connected with yourself and the other person's experience in that moment so that when they need support or reassurance, you can provide it from a place of grounding!

To successfully hold space for another, it's essential to be present with yourself first. Try not to take on their pain; focus your energy on being a support system and avoid judging either one of you - this will help unlock the healing process.

Creating a safe environment of support and understanding can be difficult, but it's an important skill when others are going through tough times. Instead of trying to "fix" someone in pain, the key is simply being present with them while they go through their journey – don't try to rush or bypass their emotions, as this will only increase feelings of isolation. Instead, practicing patience and compassion towards those you care about helps create valuable space for them, which has the potential profoundly affect how they process necessary changes during hard times.

Find yourself in need of the pure and clear attention of unconditional positive regard, and it's not available in your support system. Then, it may be time to consider finding a therapist.

NURTURE

WHAT BRINGS ME PEACE AND COMFORT

HOW TO NURTURE MY BODY

HOW TO NURTURE MY SOUL

HAPPY THINGS LIST

Challenging times can be overwhelming, but don't forget to give yourself a break every once in a while! Finding an activity that brings you happiness and comfort goes a long way toward helping you stay positive. So whether it's getting cozy for some pampering or playing your favorite sport – use this list as inspiration whenever life throws something unexpected at you; even the smallest thing can sometimes make all the difference!

WHAT IS IN MY CONTROL

THINGS TO WORK ON

THINGS I NEED TO GET RID OF (CAN'T CONTROL)

LET THAT SHIT GO

| THE THING | WHY TO LET GO? | HOW WILL IT HELP? |

GROWTH MINDSET?

Those with a growth mindset believe in unlocking their full personal potential by putting effort and investing resources into developing skills. In contrast, those with fixed mindsets believe success depends on natural ability. People who adopt a Growth Mindset strive to challenge themselves through practice and perseverance, understanding that greatness can be achieved through talent and hard work!

Are you looking to expand your potential? Cultivating a growth mindset is an empowering and life-changing journey, starting with self-reflection. First, ask yourself where you are now in personal development, then explore why it matters so much to develop this outlook. Finding other successful people who have done the same can provide inspiring insight into how they achieved transformation - failure becomes part of the learning curve rather than something feared or avoided. Finally, recognize that although ambitious goals may come at times with limitations, these should not be seen as barriers but instead opportunities for creativity and exploration while still being mindful about the language used when communicating during this process, ultimately leading to understanding brain plasticity, which will open up more possibilities on reaching one's desired objectives!

Embrace those moments of challenge and difficulty with a growth mindset! Rather than immediately assuming you can't, take some time to invest in the task at hand. Consider new things that push your boundaries, taking an action-based approach rather than one focused on traits or abilities. Reflect each day upon what didn't go as planned but remember to shift perspective - see setbacks not necessarily as failures but as valuable opportunities for learning and development. This attitude shifts reliance away from seeking external validation, so focus more on celebrating successes, both yours and others'.

Do you have a fixed or growth mindset?

Fixed Mindset
Avoids challenges.
Believes intelligence and abilities are fixed.
Effort means you're not already good enough.
Failures mean you're a failure.
Blames others for setbacks.
Becomes defensive when critiqued.
Feels threatened by other people's successes.

Growth Mindset
Embraces challenges.
Believes intelligence and abilities can be improved.
The effort helps you master new skills.
Failures are an opportunity to learn and grow.
Reflects on setbacks and uses them as lessons.
Receives feedback from others well.

GROWTH MINDSET

MY CURRENT MINDSET

GROWTH I DESIRE

HOW AM I LAGGING FROM THE GROWTH I DESIRE

WHAT IS STOPPING ME FROM BEING THAT PERSON?

SELF LOVE

THINGS I LOVE ABOUT ME

THINGS I LOVE ABOUT MY PERSONALITY

**THINGS THAT SET ME APART FROM THE CROWD:
MENTAL, PHYSICAL, OR SPIRITUAL**

THINGS I KNOW PEOPLE ADMIRE ABOUT ME

SELF LOVE

THINGS THAT MAKES ME IMPORTANT

THINGS I LOVE ABOUT MY BODY

THINGS: I MYSELF AM STRANGE AND UNUSUAL, AND THAT IS OK

**WAYS I CAN SHOW MYSELF THE SAME KINDNESS
THAT I SHOW TO OTHERS?**

IMPERFECTLY PERFECT

HOW OFTEN DO I COMPLIMENT MYSELF?

HOW OFTEN DO I CELEBRATE MY WINS?

**THINGS THAT MAKES ME INSECURE
WHAT IS THAT INNER VOICE SAYING?**

WHO VALIDATED THESE INSECURITIES?

DISCOVERY

WHAT I LIKE AND LOVE

MY TOP 3 PEOPLE I LOVE

WHAT ARE THE TRAITS THAT I LOVE IN THEM

OPINIONS

HOW CAN I JUST CHILL AND STOP WORRYING SO MUCH ABOUT WHAT OTHER PEOPLE THINK?

THREE REASONS, WHY THOSE OPINIONS SHOULD EVEN MATTER

PEOPLE WHOSE OPINIONS DON'T MATTER TO ME

PEOPLE, WHOSE OPINIONS SHOULDN'T MATTER TO ME

LIMITING BELIEFS

Challenge your perspective with a simple but powerful exercise - question the validity of limiting beliefs. First, read each statement out loud, and then ask yourself if it is true. If you realize that you don't possess concrete evidence to support your belief, this could be an opportunity for growth! Further, explore its origin by inquiring where or how I got this idea in the first place. This probing process can help identify reliable and worthwhile sources when making important decisions about our lives.

Just so you know, an expert should be someone that started where you are and then achieved what you want to achieve.

Your declaration.
Declare to yourself, **"I don't believe this anymore. It's not true."**
Now you can look for proof to show yourself that it's not true.

Imagine being free from the belief.
What would your life be like without this belief?
How would you change?
How would your life change?

Replace the belief.
You can find another belief that counteracts the old belief.
Getting rid of the limiting belief is good, but eliminating it and replacing it with something positive is even better!

Find evidence for the new belief.
Find evidence that this new belief is valid.
Keep adding evidence until you feel comfortable with the new belief.

Test yourself.
Observe your feelings, behavior, and results after replacing the belief.

Once you've eliminated the old belief and replaced it with something you like better, you'll feel and behave differently, producing more pleasing results!

AFFIRMATIONS
TO REPLACE LIMITING BELIEFS

I don't know how to do this.	I can figure it out
I'm no good at this.	As I practice, my skills will grow.
I'm not good enough.	I am valuable and worthy, and my heart is pure. The love I pour into things makes them enough.
I don't know what I want.	My higher self always knows what I want. My job is to create space to listen.
I'm too scared.	Fear is natural. I can do hard things.
I can't do a thing if someone doesn't approve.	This is my life to live, and I have to do what feels right for me.
I don't. feel confident.	It's okay to feel nervous! My confidence will grow as I practice and confront difficult things.
I might. fail!	Failure is part of success. I have to make mistakes and fail in order to succeed.
My work isn't good enough.	It doesn't have to be perfect to be wonderful.
Good things don't happen to people like me.	I am a valuable human who deserves the best.

LIMITING BELIEFS

BELIEF: IS IT WORTH IT?   **HOW TO PROGRESS**

HOW TO SET BOUNDARIES

Understand your own needs and feelings – they are the first clue that boundaries need to be set. Make sure you permit yourself to say no, without feeling like it requires any explanation or justification. Setting healthy boundaries gives you control over how others interact with you - empowering both parties for a strong relationship moving forward!
Striking the perfect balance between setting healthy boundaries and allowing for flexibility can be difficult. To find that sweet spot, it's important to become aware of your situation, so you don't veer off in either direction – too rigid leads to isolation, while being too lenient can leave one exploited instead. Give yourself grace - perfection isn't necessary here; what matters is progress toward a healthier life! And always remember: establish these guidelines with YOURSELF first; understand when something belongs only to you and protect yourself by learning to say 'that's on you' if need be.

Speak up immediately when something bothers you.

Offer up an alternative option that works better for you.

Commit to time for yourself
They are spent in ways that build you up.

Practice speaking up about little things & notice when it goes well.

Pencil yourself into your calendar. Make time for yourself in the same way you make time for others.

Find a role model (with good boundaries) and adopt some of their boundaries.

"This is hard for me, but I must be true to myself and say that I'm uncomfortable.

"That day won't work for me. Could we plan on Friday instead?"

"I'd love to hang out, but Sunday is my journaling/painting day!"

"Could I have a hug? I'm feeling a little overwhelmed right now."

"Every Thursday night, I'm going to read a couple of chapters in this self-help book that I would like to read."

"I really admire how she doesn't tolerate any backtalk. I'm going to try that for myself!"

FAMILY BOUNDARIES

Family boundaries might sound like this:
"Thank you for sharing this advice. I'll consider it and let you know when I decide."
"We have different opinions and don't have to change each other's minds.
We can agree to disagree."
"I want to spend time with you, and right now, I need some time alone to recharge."
"When you dismiss my opinions, I feel disrespected."
"I'd appreciate it if you didn't comment on my physical appearance or weight
anymore.
"When you do/say ________, it makes me feel ________."

Repeated Violation of your Boundaries:
Continue to set solid and consistent boundaries.
Record the boundary violations and your responses.
Be clear about what treatment you'll accept and what you won't.
Accept that some people will not respect your boundaries no matter what you do.
Detach from the outcome. You can't control other people.
Decide to limit or cut off all contact.

Boundaries:
If I don't like how you speak to me, I won't allow you to talk to me anymore.
If I don't like how you deal with me, I won't allow you to deal with me anymore.
If I don't like how I feel around you, I won't allow myself to be in that position
anymore.
If I can't change these things, I will remind myself that your behavior is a reflection of
you, not me.

Boundaries with yourself look like this:
I will silence my phone in the evenings and while I sleep.
I will check in with myself to ensure alignment before I agree to anything.
I will nourish my body and mind with loving and high-vibrational foods and thoughts.
I will notice when I need to rest, and I create space to relax and nurture myself- guilt-
free.
I will notice when something drains my energy, and I no longer engage with it.
I will notice when something no longer aligns and let it go with love and grace.
Finally, I will commit to my daily health/healing/spiritual practices.

BOUNDARIES

ARE:
Communicating what you will
and will not do.

Honoring yourself and what you need
to be the best YOU.

Preventative actions so you
remain balanced.

Clarifying how you will respond in
certain situations.

ARE NOT:
Giving someone an
ultimatum.

Selfish! They exist so you can show up
better for yourself and others.

Stonewalling without warning
or explanation.

Requesting someone to change
their behavior.

BOUNDARIES

I'm aware of my needs
(physical, spiritual,
emotional)

I say no to things that
are out of alignment or
don't serve me

I connect with people
when I am emotionally
open to connect

I am not made to feel
"in the middle" of family
conflict or issues

I generally don't feel
resentment within
my relationships

LACK OF BOUNDARIES

I lack awareness of my
needs + often feel burnt
out + not appreciated

I say "yes" to avoid
feeling guilty or not
getting approval

I feel pressured to
immediately respond
+ rarely take space

People in my family
involve me in conflict
or "taking sides"

I feel resentment or
like I'm being taken
advantage of often

THINGS TO SAY

Things to Say to Set Boundaries

"I wish I could help, but I'm not available right now to support you."
"I can't commit to that right now. Can we work to find a compromise?"
"I have made up my mind about this."
"I don't discuss this matter."
"I trust that you will be able to find a solution to this problem."
"I have nothing planned, but that doesn't mean I'm available."
"I need some time and space to think this through."
"I hope you will find a way to solve this problem."
"I'm not able to take on additional work right now."
"I'm not interested in talking about that person when they're not here."

Difficult Family Members

Only try to fix them if you see they're making an effort to listen and meet you halfway and temper your expectations for change.

Be present and direct. Someone trying to stir up conflict can easily set you off. Be direct and assertive. If a talk becomes about "winning," end it.

Encourage them to express themselves. Let them fully state their point of view without interruption. Stay as neutral as possible.

Watch for trigger topics. Be prepared to address them in a non-confrontational way and to change the topic if necessary.

It's not about you, usually. But unfortunately, arguments can quickly expand to personal attacks. Try to imagine it unfolding before it does and nip it in the bud.

Your well-being comes first. Plan ahead and avoid getting stuck alone with them. No one is entitled to occupy your space unless you let them in.

WHAT BOUNDARIES SOUND LIKE

It's not my responsibility to make sure others are responsible.

It's not my job to rescue people from their drama.

It is okay if others get angry.

It's okay to say No.

It's my job to make myself happy and discover what brings me joy.

It's not my job to think, feel, or live for others.

I have a right to feel my feelings no matter what anyone else thinks about my feelings.

No one has to agree with me.

No one has a right to verbally abuse me, including family, friends, partners, and coworkers.

It's not okay to enmesh with my thoughts, emotions, or other people.

It's okay to spend time alone without explaining myself.

I do not need permission to be who I am and think what I think.

Other people have every right to dislike or disagree with me, but they do not have the right to disrespect me.

I have a right to end draining conversations and relationships.

I know I am enough.

Live your life!
You Do You, Boo!

Remember: Your energy is a precious commodity for only those special few who truly appreciate your worth. You possess something rare and valuable; use it wisely to make sure you surround yourself with people who understand its value and help your spirit shine even brighter. Your inner glow has been growing ever since the moment of creation - acknowledging this now will allow you to tap into that source of power so you can reach goals beyond anything imaginable!

MY BOUNDARIES

WHO- WHAT- HOW

DATE: ______________

STRATEGIES AND IDEAS

SHORT-TERM STRATEGIES

Negative emotions can be a real challenge, but you don't have to let them take over. Here are some short-term strategies that might help: Distract yourself by focusing on something else; try doing an activity that needs your full attention and makes you forget what upset you first! Then, interrupt those negative patterns with silly or unusual activities like shouting out loud or dancing around - it's really effective for changing your mindset quickly. Moving is another excellent way of managing stress; standing up, walking outside, doing push-ups...anything physical will make all the difference when dealing with tough emotions. And if music helps calm things down, too – why not throw on one of your favorite tunes?

If you're feeling overwhelmed, take a step back and let yourself feel the emotions. Writing down your worries can help you focus on what is causing stress and identify how it should be addressed. Discussing these feelings with someone impartial may provide valuable insight that turns anxiety into clarity. Make sure to prioritize rest as well; fatigue amplifies worry, so never underestimate the power of good sleep! Finally, don't forget about breathwork — slow breaths bring mental and physical balance during difficult times, while energizing techniques will increase capabilities for tackling whatever comes next!

Take a short break to re-center and rejuvenate! Start by releasing tension from your facial muscles, then move down the body. Try taking slow breaths in through the nose and out through the mouth while allowing your mind to relax and flow into a state of peace. In no time, you'll feel more physically and emotionally relaxed – ready for whatever life throws you next!

LONG-TERM STRATEGIES

Want to break free from negative emotions once and for all? Long-term strategies will help you stay on the right path. Here are two techniques that can assist in your journey:

First, take time to uncover what lies beneath – writing down why these feelings exist and how they were triggered is a great place to start. Then see if it's possible to let emotions go by releasing this story as an author of one's own life.

Second - keep track daily! A journal dedicated entirely to documenting emotional states allows reflecting upon recurring patterns and relevant affirmations or exercises, ensuring long-lasting success when overcoming them.

Create positive habits and reduce the negative! Take time to practice mindfulness so you can observe your emotions throughout the day. Meditation is an excellent way of doing this, as well as engaging in activities while being fully present - noticing what's happening inside yourself. In addition, be mindful of who or what surrounds you; if it doesn't add anything meaningful to your life, step away from it for a while or make some changes. Finally, taking control by removing unnecessary distractions like too much TV watching or internet browsing will help bring balance back into focus and allow long-term strategies to flourish!

Incorporate long-term strategies into your daily routine for a more joyous and energized life. Establish rituals such as meditating, exercising, and repeating affirmations to nurture positive emotions. Make sure to get enough sleep by going to bed at the same time each day; this helps encourage mental and physical health while providing vital energy throughout the following day!

Consult a professional: if you have deep emotional issues such as extremely low self-esteem or depression, it might be wise to consult a professional.

I DON'T KNOW WHO NEEDS TO HEAR THIS BUT...

Let That Shit Go!

Worrying about what has happened in the past.
The need to be in control of everything.
The idea of a "perfect life."
Fear of the unknown.
Unhealthy relationships.
Worrying about things out of your control.
The clothing you haven't worn in over a year.
A job you hate.
Overscheduling your life.
Comparing yourself to other people.
Placing your partner on an unrealistic pedestal.
Going small when you can go BIG.
Your insecurities.
A negative body image.
Fear of failure.
Clutter in your home.
Procrastinating on important things.
Overspending.
Your pride.

Worrying what others think of you.
Excuses.
Your dependency on social media.
Your comfort zone.
Failing to care for your physical health.
Grudges.
Lazy habits that are holding you back.
Past debts.
The belief that the "grass is always greener."
Gossip.
Guilt and anger over past events.
Any possessions that don't bring you joy.
Unrealistic expectations.
Trying to make everyone happy.
Old things you can donate or sell for cash.
Overindulging in unhealthy habits.
Jealousy.
Anyone and anything that doesn't make you happy.

REMEMBER
My past does not define me.
I am a stronger person for facing my emotions.
I am choosing to accept my past for what it is.
I accept and love my true self as I am.
I forgive myself for my mistakes.
I forgive others who have treated me poorly.

I am not going to go all Carl Jung on you, but if you are interested in digging deep, then prepare for a rough ride because healing hurts; otherwise, everyone would do it:-)

Take a moment to pause, check-in, and focus on your self-care before going through the upcoming prompts. It is okay if you find yourself struggling with some questions or feeling disconnected; allow yourself time to process while being kind and gentle with yourself along the way. To make it as easy as possible for readers, this book has been divided into three different sections beginning with childhood memories - don't worry if there are pages here that do not pertain directly to you – feel free to skip them!

It is also okay to skip over certain pages because you have a **"NOT TODAY SATAN"** moment. Just come back when you feel like you can continue.

Ready? Okay, go grab your notebook because I didn't add extra note pages because it would be way too thick., pen or pencil, and maybe a piece of smoky quartz, and let's do this.

Got it? Now find a quiet place to get comfortable, wherever you feel happy and safe; maybe light some candles, grab a pillow and blanket, and plop yourself down.

SCARS
PROVE
THAT YOU
ARE STILL HERE
SO LET'S PEEK
AT WHERE THEY CAME
FROM.

IT IS
EASIER TO BUILD
UP A CHILD THAN IT IS
TO REPAIR AN ADULT.

~Frederick Douglass

MY AFFIRMATIONS

DATE: _________________

WHAT DO I WANT TO GET OUT OF SHADOW WORK?

MY HAPPY THOUGHTS

Here are some journaling prompts for working through emotion that you might ask yourself.

What is this emotion called? Can I name it?
Is this my emotion or somebody else's?
Where does it live in my body?
S0, if I was describing this emotion to someone else. Does it have texture? Color? A temperature? A shape?
Why do I think this mention has come to visit?
Where might this emotion have originated from?
Does this emotion have a message for me?
Does this emotion want me to take any particular next step?
What would I like to say back to this emotion?
How can I thank this mention for its wisdom?

10 MINUTE
AM and PM Rituals

GROUNDING
Takes: 1-2 minutes
Pick One: Body scan, Mindfulness, or Meditation

BRAIN VOMIT
Takes: 1-2 minutes
Write out anything flooding your mind without any filter or need for what you write to be meaningful. Just let it out!

PLAN AHEAD
Takes: 3 minutes
If it's morning time, make a list of what you need to get done today, then figure out which tasks are most important. That way, you'll know where to start.

If it's evening time, list what you need to get done tomorrow, then figure out which tasks are most important. That way, you'll know where to start.

TALK TO ME
Takes: 2-3 minutes
Make 4-6 affirmations about any of the following: abilities, skills, safety, or stress management.

I often wonder about who I was as a child. I am told I was very outgoing and fun, but now I am a shy, reserved person who loves spending time alone. How did I change, or what changed me?

Describe yourself as a child.
What was I like?

How have I changed from that child?

How do I think I was seen as a child?

Was that a true representation of myself? Why or why not?

Who do I compare myself to most often?
Why do I think that is?

WHAT HAVE YOU DISCOVERED

LLL
Life Lessons Learned

1. _______________________

2. _______________________

3. _______________________

Gold Star Moments

1. _______________________

2. _______________________

3. _______________________

Vomit Bucket
Things That Still Needs Work

Things To Be Released

1. _______________________

2. _______________________

3. _______________________

REWARD:_______________________

Write down 7 compliments that people have given to me as a child.

Describe what my bedroom looked like as a child.

What did I want to be as a child? Why? How did that change?

What were my dreams and goals as a child?

Did I reach them?
Why or why not?

When and how did they change?

What stories did I enjoy as a child? Why?

What was my favorite activity as a child?

How did this activity bring me joy?

Do I still do this activity? Why or why not?

As a child, I would daydream about what?

As a child, I always wondered about what?

As a child I was fascinated by what?

What is your best childhood memory and why?

What messages did I get about who I was or who I was supposed to be?

How did that differ from what I wanted?
How did that make me feel?

Who was responsible for these messages?
How has that affected me going forward?

What music did I listen to as a child? Do I still listen to it?

Are there any songs that framed my childhood?

Are there any songs that I refuse to listen to from my childhood? Why?

WHAT HAVE YOU DISCOVERED

LLL
Life Lessons Learned

1. _______________________________

____

2. _______________________________

____

3. _______________________________

____

____

____

____

____

Gold Star Moments

1. _______________________________

____

2. _______________________________

____

3. _______________________________

Vomit Bucket
Things That Still Needs Work

____

____

____

____

____

____

Things To Be Released

1. _______________________________

____

2. _______________________________

____

3. _______________________________

____

____

____

____

____

____

____

____

REWARD: _______________________________

Hey, it's me. I'm checking in to see how you're doing.

I know this stuff can be tough to deal with sometimes. You might feel overwhelmed, but it's important to remember that you're making progress. You're learning more about yourself daily and working towards your goal of forgiveness and acceptance.

YOU'RE DOING A FANTASTIC JOB!

Looking back on my childhood, I can see how various experiences and people shaped who I am today.

What was my first experience with success?

What was my first experience with failure?

Write down a few memories of when I felt truly peaceful during my childhood.

Do I consider these my best memories as a child? Why or why not?

Write down 1 or 2 memories about times when life surprised me in a fascinating way during my childhood.

What was my favorite show, book, game, or comic? Why?

How was my childhood?
Describe it.

What could have made it better?

WHAT HAVE YOU DISCOVERED

LLL
Life Lessons Learned

1. _______________________________

____

2. _______________________________

____

3. _______________________________

____

____

____

____

____

Gold Star Moments

1. _______________________________

____

2. _______________________________

____

3. _______________________________

Vomit Bucket
Things That Still Needs Work

____

____

____

____

____

____

____

____

Things To Be Released

1. _______________________________

____

2. _______________________________

____

3. _______________________________

____

____

____

____

REWARD:_______________________________

What is my saddest memory from my childhood? Describe it.

Did it shape me as an adult?

Does it still affect me today in the same way? Why or why not?

Why do I think that is?

What was my biggest worry as a child? Why?

Do I still have this worry(ies) today

What were my caregivers' biggest worries when I was a child?

I have always suppressed my emotions and never allowed myself to figure out what was making me feel shameful and regretful.

Do I have any shameful memories of my childhood? Things that I couldn't talk about to anyone?

Do any of these memories still bother me today? If so, why?

How might this shame still be affecting me now?

Have I talked about them as an adult?

As children, we all did some shameful things that we now feel regret; list some.

Based on this list, what is the worst thing I did and regret?

Based on this list, which memory do I not want to remember?

Based on this list, which memory do I not want other people to know?

____

____

____

____

____

____

____

____

____

____

____

____

____

____

____

____

____

____

____

____

____

WHAT HAVE YOU DISCOVERED

LLL
Life Lessons Learned

1. __________________________

____

2. __________________________

____

3. __________________________

____

____

____

____

____

Gold Star Moments

1. __________________________

____

2. __________________________

____

3. __________________________

Vomit Bucket
Things That Still Needs Work

____

____

____

____

____

____

Things To Be Released

1. __________________________

____

2. __________________________

____

3. __________________________

____

____

____

____

____

____

REWARD:__________________________

Hi there!

I just wanted to see how you're doing. You've made so much progress, and I'm really proud of you. I know you can achieve anything you set your mind to. So, if you're feeling a little down, why not go outside and take in the nature around you? Breathe in peace, and with each calm breath, breathe out stress and tension, stretch and relax your body.

YOU ARE INCREDIBLE!

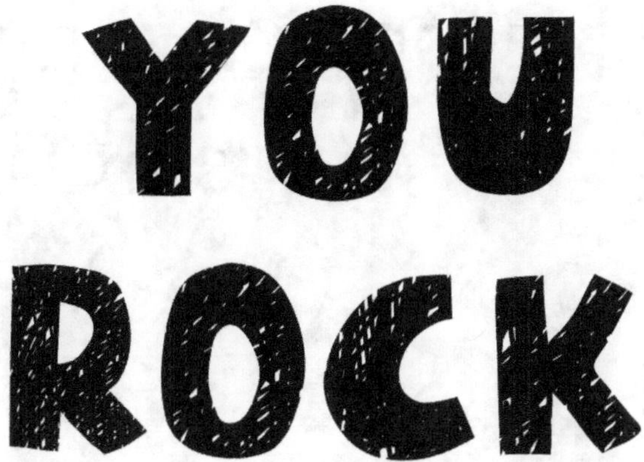

It's not hard to figure out
when exactly I started feeling
fearful over many things and
hyper-vigilant this way.

If it looks right but feels wrong,
it's FEAR.
If it looks wrong but feels right,
it's INTUITION.

What are some of the causes for my feelings of happiness growing up?

What are some of the causes for my feelings of sadness growing up?

When I was a child, was I afraid of the dark?

If so, look deep and try to find the root or cause of my fear of the dark.

If not, describe when I felt fearful and afraid.

Now look deep and try to find the root or cause of that fear.

When I was fearful and afraid, how did I react then?

WHAT HAVE YOU DISCOVERED

LLL
Life Lessons Learned

1. _______________________________

   ____
2. _______________________________

   ____
3. _______________________________

   ____

   ____

   ____

   ____

   ____

Gold Star Moments

1. _______________________________

   ____
2. _______________________________

   ____
3. _______________________________

Vomit Bucket
Things That Still Needs Work

____

____

____

____

____

____

____

____

____

____

____

Things To Be Released

1. _______________________________

   ____
2. _______________________________

   ____
3. _______________________________

   ____

REWARD: _______________________________

When I felt hurt, how did I react then?

When I felt fearful, afraid, or hurt, how did my caregiver(s) address those emotions?

How did their reaction make me feel at the time?

Does it still affect me today in the same way?
Why or why not?

Have I overcome this fear? Why or why not? What would it take to conquer it?

What else made me afraid as a child? Why?

What did I fear most as a child? Why do I think that is?

How and when did each of these fears begin?

Have I overcome this fear? Why or why not? What would it take to conquer it?

WHAT HAVE YOU DISCOVERED

LLL
Life Lessons Learned

1. _______________________________

2. _______________________________
   ____

3. _______________________________
   ____
   ____
   ____
   ____
   ____

Gold Star Moments

1. _______________________________
   ____

2. _______________________________
   ____

3. _______________________________

Vomit Bucket
Things That Still Needs Work

____
____
____
____
____
____
____
____
____
____
____

Things To Be Released

1. _______________________________
   ____

2. _______________________________
   ____

3. _______________________________
   ____

REWARD:_______________________________

Did anything happen to me that was life-changing? Describe.

How did this incident influence me as I was growing older? Why?

I was constantly
torn between what I
was expected to do
and what I wanted
to do
as I grew older.

When I was a kid, loneliness meant feeling like I didn't belong anywhere. I would try to escape it by reading books. How about you?

Did I ever feel abandoned as a child?

Describe when did I feel abandoned as a child?

What can I say to that version of me who felt abandoned?

WHAT HAVE YOU DISCOVERED

LLL
Life Lessons Learned

1. _______________________

____

2. _______________________

____

3. _______________________

____

____

____

____

____

Gold Star Moments

1. _______________________

____

2. _______________________

____

3. _______________________

Vomit Bucket
Things That Still Needs Work

____

____

____

____

____

____

____

____

Things To Be Released

1. _______________________

____

2. _______________________

____

3. _______________________

____

REWARD:_______________________

When did I learn about emotions as a child?

What made me angry as a child? Why?

Do I still have the same anger today?

What negative emotion did I not want to feel as a child? What do I think is the reason behind this?

Were there any emotions that were off-limits? Which ones?

List any emotions I have felt on one side of the page, and on the other side of the page, list the ones I wasn't allowed to express during my childhood.

What were the emotions? What would happen if I showed those emotions?

How did I learn not to show those emotions?

Can I show those emotions now? Why or why not?

How did I usually process my emotions as a child, whether they were positive or negative?

WHAT HAVE YOU DISCOVERED

LLL
Life Lessons Learned

1. ___________________________
   ____
2. ___________________________
   ____
3. ___________________________
   ____
   ____
   ____
   ____
   ____

Gold Star Moments

1. ___________________________
   ____
2. ___________________________
   ____
3. ___________________________

Vomit Bucket
Things That Still Needs Work

____
____
____
____
____
____
____
____
____
____
____
____

Things To Be Released

1. ___________________________
   ____
2. ___________________________
   ____
3. ___________________________
   ____

REWARD: ___________________________

Looking back, have I noticed any changes I made over time as I got older?

What are those changes?

Looking back, have I noticed any changes others have made over time as I got older?

What are those changes that others made?

What primary coping strategy(s) did I develop as a child?

Do I still use them to this day?

What communication patterns did I develop as a child?

Do I still use them today?

Hey,
I'm checking in to see how you're doing. You've come so far, and I'm really proud of you. I know you might feel a little shaky right now, but why not do something on your list that will make you happy?

YOU DESERVE IT!

INNER CHILD TRAUMA

REJECTION TRAUMA

MAY LOOK LIKE

You easily make negative assumptions about what others are thinking
You worry about letting people in
You find compromising difficult
You are a people pleaser

SPEAK INTO EXISTENCE

Positive energy nourishes my body and helps me to radiate joy to others.
A happy, joyful life is being created for me right now.

ABANDONMENT TRAUMA

MAY LOOK LIKE

Feel of being left behind or abandoned
Inability to form healthy relationships in the teenage years and adulthood.

SPEAK INTO EXISTENCE

All of my words, thoughts, and actions are divinely guided and protected
The universe will guide me on anything and everything divinely

BETRAYAL TRAUMA

MAY LOOK LIKE

Trouble recognizing, expressing, or managing emotions.
Anxiety, depression, and other mental health symptoms issues
Nightmares
Panic attacks

SPEAK INTO EXISTENCE

Every challenge I face is an opportunity to grow and improve
My contributions are unique and meaningful

INJUSTICE TRAUMA

MAY LOOK LIKE

Chronica chest and back pain
Feeling fatigued or drained
Unpredictable and irrational emotions
Disassociation and short attention span

SPEAK INTO EXISTENCE

I deserve to feel safe, comfortable, and confident in this body
I accept myself the way I am, my body is perfect the way it is.

INNER CHILD WOUNDS

GUILT WOUND
Feels "sorry" or "bad"
Doesn't like to ask for things
Uses guilt to manipulate
Is afraid to set boundaries
Normally attracts people who make them feel guilty

TRUST WOUND
Is afraid to be hurt
Doesn't trust themselves
Finds ways not to trust people
Feels insecure and needs lots of external validation
Doesn't feel safe
Normally attracts people who don't feel safe

NEGLECT WOUND
Struggles to let things go
Has low self-worth
Gets angry easily
Struggles to say no
Represses emotions
Shies away from being vulnerable
Normally attracts people who don't appreciate them or make them feel "seen"
Easily make negative assumptions about what others are thinking
Have a hard time trusting people with your feelings

Do I remember a traumatic experience from my childhood? Describe it.

How did I react at the time?

How did my caregiver(s) respond?

How did their reaction make me feel at the time?

Does it still affect me today in the same way?

It's okay to make mistakes.
We all do it.
What's important is that you learn from them and
don't hold yourself back because of them.
It's time to forgive yourself
and let go of whatever is holding you back
so you can move on with your life.

YOU DESERVE IT!!!

Write down what's holding me back and why I need to forgive myself. Then, get all your emotions out and let yourself feel forgiveness. You deserve it.

What is the one thing I can't bring myself to let go of from my childhood?

How have I changed from that child?

Were the change for the better or worse?

What caused me to change?

Do I miss the child that I was?

Describe who or what changed me.

Did someone or something negatively influence that decision? How?

I was always misunderstood and considered to have a chip on my shoulder as I was growing up. I just could not express myself properly, so I expressed myself through self-harm and anger.

Write down a few defining moments where I tried to speak up but were shut down.

Who shut me down?

How did I feel when I was shut down?

What was the result of being shut down?

Do I remember being misunderstood when I was a child? Describe it.

How did I react then?

How did my caregiver(s) respond?

How did their reaction make me feel at the time?

WHAT HAVE YOU DISCOVERED

LLL
Life Lessons Learned

1. _______________________________

____

2. _______________________________

____

3. _______________________________

____

____

____

____

____

Gold Star Moments

1. _______________________________

____

2. _______________________________

____

3. _______________________________

Vomit Bucket
Things That Still Needs Work

____

____

____

____

____

____

____

____

____

____

____

____

____

Things To Be Released

1. _______________________________

____

2. _______________________________

____

3. _______________________________

____

REWARD:_______________________________

What made me start doubting myself as a kid?

Was it a person, an event, a place, or a specific instance?

Would I want to change my upbringing, childhood, or what happened to me? Damn skippy, I would! Now, after making this book, I don't know

What do I wish you could change about my childhood? Why?

If I could go back and change it, would I? Or did it teach me a valuable life lesson?

If I did go back and change that one thing, how would it have impacted you as a child?

If I did go back and change that one thing, how would it impact me today? For better or worse?

What is my worst memory as a child? Describe it.

Why is this my worst memory?

How did I react then?

How did my caregiver(s) respond?

How did their reaction make me feel at the time?

Does it still affect me today in the same way? Why or why not?

Hi There!

I am so thrilled that you are still here. You're terrific, and you are doing so great! You got this! If you're feeling unsure, why not use your affirmation list? If you didn't do one, maybe today is the day to make one.

I can do this

I am brave

I am loved

I believe in me

When I reflect on my life, I sometimes find myself questioning if I should be grateful for what I have instead of what I didn't have.

WHAT HAVE YOU DISCOVERED

LLL
Life Lessons Learned

1. ___________________________
   ____
2. ___________________________
   ____
3. ___________________________
   ____
   ____
   ____
   ____
   ____

Gold Star Moments

1. ___________________________
   ____
2. ___________________________
   ____
3. ___________________________

Vomit Bucket
Things That Still Needs Work

____
____
____
____
____
____
____
____
____
____
____
____
____

Things To Be Released

1. ___________________________
   ____
2. ___________________________
   ____
3. ___________________________
   ____

REWARD: ___________________________

Did I have my basic needs met?
(shelter, food, water, clothing, and safety)

Why or Why not?
What was missing?

How did I feel if and when my needs weren't met?

Was I cared for well?

An emotional need is a state or condition that must be fulfilled to experience happiness and peace. When our emotional needs are met and responded to appropriately, they keep us in balance. They are essential to a healthy lifestyle.

We may feel frustrated, hurt, or dissatisfied when they aren't addressed.

Though we all have them, everyone has unique emotional needs. The differences may result from our upbringing, culture, genetic predisposition, sense of identity, the current phase of life or age, and other individual factors.

Did I have your emotional needs met? (love, affection, acceptance, trust, validation, protection, and attention)

Why or Why not?
What was missing?

How did it feel if and when my needs weren't met?

I have often considered whether I was responsible for my own safety or if some of my caretakers should have had this responsibility.

What situations always made me feel uncomfortable? Describe them.

How did I react to them at that time?

Do they still affect me today in the same way? Why or why not?

What is my definition of being safe?

What would it have taken for me to feel safe as a child?

Describe the feeling of being safe.

What made me feel safe as a child?
(person, place, thing or activity)

Do I still have that safe person, place, thing, or activity today?

If not, what happened to it?

Did I ever feel safe after it was gone?
Why or why not?

Hey there!
If you're feeling down, remember that you can achieve anything you set your mind to. So keep going! And if you need a little help, why not make a self-soothe box?
If you don't have one, maybe today is the day to make one.

WHAT HAVE YOU DISCOVERED

LLL
Life Lessons Learned

1. _______________________________

____

2. _______________________________

____

3. _______________________________

____

____

____

____

Gold Star Moments

1. _______________________________

____

2. _______________________________

____

3. _______________________________

Vomit Bucket
Things That Still Needs Work

____

____

____

____

____

____

Things To Be Released

1. _______________________________

____

2. _______________________________

____

3. _______________________________

____

____

____

____

____

____

REWARD:_______________________________

Throughout your life, you might have developed certain self-limiting beliefs based on things that happened to you in your childhood

Write about an experience that started my self-limiting beliefs or insecurities (such as fear of failure or not feeling good enough)

____
____
____
____
____
____
____
____
____
____
____
____
____
____
____
____
____
____
____
____
____

Did that shape me in any way as an adult? Why?

What was the result or outcome of these beliefs?

Do I still hold these beliefs today?

Who was the first person who made me feel insecure?

Who has hurt me in the past?

What would I say to them now if I could?

WHAT HAVE YOU DISCOVERED

LLL
Life Lessons Learned

1. _______________________
____
2. _______________________
____
3. _______________________
____
____
____
____
____

Gold Star Moments

1. _______________________
____
2. _______________________
____
3. _______________________

Vomit Bucket
Things That Still Needs Work

____
____
____
____
____
____
____
____
____
____
____
____

Things To Be Released

1. _______________________
____
2. _______________________
____
3. _______________________
____

REWARD: _______________________

What's an early childhood memory that has stuck with me into adulthood? Describe it.

Why do I think this memory has followed you into adulthood?

Asking ourselves
why we seek
attention and from
whom, whether it is
good or bad
attention, can help
us understand how
that has affected us
or if this still lingers
in our lives.

Did I know the difference between pleasing people and being genuinely kind?

Did I receive enough attention as a child?

Who gave me their attention?

Who didn't give me their attention?

Why do I think that they didn't give you attention?

How did I feel when you wanted attention?

How did I feel when I didn't get the attention I was seeking?

How did I react when I didn't get their attention?

Did it shape me as an adult?

WHAT HAVE YOU DISCOVERED

LLL
Life Lessons Learned

1. ______________________________

____

2. ______________________________

____

3. ______________________________

____

____

____

____

____

Gold Star Moments

1. ______________________________

____

2. ______________________________

____

3. ______________________________

Vomit Bucket
Things That Still Needs Work

____

____

____

____

____

____

____

____

____

____

____

____

____

____

Things To Be Released

1. ______________________________

____

2. ______________________________

____

3. ______________________________

____

REWARD: ______________________________

What methods did
you find most
effective in seeking
comfort or were
most effective in
providing you
comfort as a child?

What habits in my childhood gave me a feeling of comfort?

Do I still have those habits today?

Did I receive comfort as a child?

Who comforted me, and how was I comforted as a child?

Did my caregiver(s) give me comfort?

How did I comfort myself when I was a child?

How do I comfort myself now that I am an adult?

WHAT HAVE YOU DISCOVERED

LLL
Life Lessons Learned

1. _______________________________

____

2. _______________________________

____

3. _______________________________

____

____

____

____

____

Gold Star Moments

1. _______________________________

____

2. _______________________________

____

3. _______________________________

Vomit Bucket
Things That Still Needs Work

____

____

____

____

____

____

____

____

____

____

____

____

Things To Be Released

1. _______________________________

____

2. _______________________________

____

3. _______________________________

____

REWARD: _______________________________

Did anything "big" happen in my home? Describe it.

Was there open communication when something "big" happened in my home?

How did I react to the "big thing" happening?

How did my caregiver(s) respond to the "big thing" happening?

How did their reaction make me feel at the time?

Does it still affect me today in the same way?

Were there secrets or things I hid from outside of my home?
(church, school, or other family members)

What were those secrets or things?

Why do I think they were not spoken of?

Who told me not to speak of these things?

To this day, have they ever been spoken? Why or why not?

Did others ever find them out?

If not, what do I think would happen if you spoke about them now?

What happened in my home that I knew about, but no one outside my family did?

Did they ever find out? How?

WHAT HAVE YOU DISCOVERED

LLL
Life Lessons Learned

1. _______________________________

____

2. _______________________________

____

3. _______________________________

____

____

____

____

Gold Star Moments

1. _______________________________

____

2. _______________________________

____

3. _______________________________

Vomit Bucket
Things That Still Needs Work

____

____

____

____

____

____

____

____

____

____

____

____

____

Things To Be Released

1. _______________________________

____

2. _______________________________

____

3. _______________________________

____

REWARD: _______________________________

It's really weird how you can actually feel it in your chest and stomach when something or someone really hurts your feelings.

Remember:
It hurt because it mattered.

I wish I could give you my pain just for one moment. Not to hurt you, but so that you could finally understand how much you hurt me.

Who hurt me the most in my childhood?

How did they hurt me?

How did I react to it?

How did my caregiver(s) respond to it?

How did their reaction make me feel?

Does it still affect me today in the same way?
Why or why not?

Have I forgiven them?

If not, why?

WHAT HAVE YOU DISCOVERED

LLL
Life Lessons Learned

1. _______________________

____

2. _______________________

____

3. _______________________

____

____

____

____

Gold Star Moments

1. _______________________

____

2. _______________________

____

3. _______________________

Vomit Bucket
Things That Still Needs Work

____

____

____

____

____

____

____

____

____

____

____

Things To Be Released

1. _______________________

____

2. _______________________

____

3. _______________________

____

REWARD:_______________________

The collective unconscious is a unique component in that Carl Jung believed that this part of the psyche served as a form of psychological inheritance. It contained all the knowledge and experiences humans share as a species. Jung rejected the concept of tabula rasa or the notion that the human mind is a blank slate at birth, to be written solely by experience. Instead, he believed that the human mind retains fundamental, unconscious, biological aspects of our ancestors. These "primordial images," as he initially dubbed them, serve as a basic foundation for being human.

Jung believed that each archetype played a role in personality but felt that most people were dominated by one specific archetype. According to Jung, how an archetype is expressed or realized depends upon several factors, including an individual's cultural influences and personal experiences.

Jung identified four major archetypes but also believed there was no limit to the number that may exist. The existence of these archetypes cannot be observed directly but can be inferred by looking at religion, dreams, art, and literature.

The Persona
The Shadow
The Anima or Animus
The Self

Jung acknowledged that the four main archetypes could intermingle and give rise to 12 archetypical figures (also known as archetypical images). These include:

Ruler - control
Creator/artist - innovation
Sage - understanding
Innocent - safety
Explorer - freedom
Outlaw - liberation
Hero - mastery
Magician - power
Jester - enjoyment
Everyman - belonging
Lover - intimacy
Caregiver - service

List some of the worst personality traits or flaws with which I personally interacted.

Did I see any of these traits in people that I knew as a child?

Did I see any of these traits in my caregiver(s) as a child?

Did I have any of these traits when I was younger?

Do I still have any of these traits?

Many things influenced me during my childhood, and looking back on them now, I can see how they shaped me as a person.

Remember, you have no idea the number of people that God/Universe/Source may want to influence through you.

No matter who you are or what you do, you always have the potential to positively affect others.

Write down 1 or 2 experiences from my childhood that changed how I see myself.

List some of the people I looked up to while growing up.

Who had the biggest influence on me as a child?

Describe each one and write why I felt that way.

Did any of them influence me in any way?

How and why?

WHAT HAVE YOU DISCOVERED

LLL
Life Lessons Learned

1. ___________________________

____

2. ___________________________

____

3. ___________________________

____

____

____

____

____

Gold Star Moments

1. ___________________________

____

2. ___________________________

____

3. ___________________________

Vomit Bucket
Things That Still Needs Work

____

____

____

____

____

____

____

____

____

____

____

____

____

____

Things To Be Released

1. ___________________________

____

2. ___________________________

____

3. ___________________________

____

REWARD:___________________________

I don't trust words; I trust vibes.
People can tell you anything,
but a vibe tells you everything.

I don't trust words.
I even question actions.
But I never doubt patterns.

Trust takes years to build,
seconds to break,
and forever to repair.

Relationships are built on trust...Was my trust ever broken as a child? Explain?

How did I react at that time?

How did my caregiver(s) respond?

How did their reaction make me feel then?

Does it still affect me today in the same way? Why or why not?

Has any good come out of it?

What would I say to them today if I could?

What did it take for them to gain my trust afterward? If they did.

In what ways have all these things affected my life now?

WHAT HAVE YOU DISCOVERED

LLL
Life Lessons Learned

1. _______________________

   ____

2. _______________________

   ____

3. _______________________

   ____

   ____

   ____

   ____

   ____

Gold Star Moments

1. _______________________

   ____

2. _______________________

   ____

3. _______________________

Vomit Bucket
Things That Still Needs Work

____

____

____

____

____

____

____

Things To Be Released

1. _______________________

   ____

2. _______________________

   ____

3. _______________________

   ____

____

____

____

____

____

____

REWARD:_______________________

I have a really hard time asking for help, so if I told you I needed you, I really did, and if you weren't there when I needed you, I probably won't ask again.

When did someone surprise me, despite mydoubts about him or her?

Write down three memories where God/Source/Higher Power/Universe really helped me in a surprising way?

____

____

____

____

____

____

____

____

____

____

____

____

____

____

____

____

____

____

____

____

____

Make a list of moments when other people helped me through difficult times.

Did I ever ask for help from an adult?

What did I ask for help with?

Who did I ask for help?

What happened when I asked for help?

What was their response?
(disbelief, anger, ignored or validation)

How did their reaction make me feel at the time?

Does it still affect me today in the same way? Why or why not?

Write my caregiver(s) a letter. What do I want to say to them? This could be positive or negative.

WHAT HAVE YOU DISCOVERED

LLL
Life Lessons Learned

1. _______________________________

____

2. _______________________________

____

3. _______________________________

____

____

____

____

Gold Star Moments

1. _______________________________

____

2. _______________________________

____

3. _______________________________

Vomit Bucket
Things That Still Needs Work

____

____

____

____

____

____

____

____

____

____

____

____

Things To Be Released

1. _______________________________

____

2. _______________________________

____

3. _______________________________

____

REWARD:_______________________________

I suffer from nightmares and night terrors, so I find these quotes profoundly moving.

Nightmares are just free horror movies that you produce, direct, and star in.

My best dreams and worst nightmares have the same people in them.
~ Philippos

Chase your dreams, and your nightmares will grow tired of chasing you.
~Matshona Dhliwayo

Have I ever been plagued by the same nightmare over and over again? Think back to what was going on in your life when these dreams started. Describe it.

My dreams can often be a reflection of something going on in my life that I'm not even aware of. It's possible that my nightmares are a sign that there's something going on that I'm still trying to ignore or avoid.

I shouldn't let things bother me, but I do.

It is crazy how you being unbothered, bother people.

What is something that happened in my childhood that still bothers me?

What lesson from childhood has stuck with me the most? Why?

What communication patterns did I develop as a child?

What primary coping strategy did I develop as a child that I still use now?

What would I like people to understand about me and my childhood?

What was my main cause(s) for my feelings of unhappiness during my childhood?

How is the way I was raised helping you today?

How is the way I was raised hurting me today?

What would the 7-year-old version of myself think about you today?

What would I create if I were given a blank page upon which I could recreate my life?

What does my shadow look like?

What would happen if I made peace with my shadow side and embraced it as part of who I am?

What advice would I give to myself as a child and teenager?

Is a childhood wound still running my life?

What could be the next step toward accepting and fixing it?

What would that person look like if I met the hurt part of myself?

What would they tell me?

What would I tell them?

What pain did I encounter as a child that was a blessing in disguise?

How and why?

WHAT HAVE YOU DISCOVERED

LLL
Life Lessons Learned

1. _______________________
   ____
2. _______________________
   ____
3. _______________________
   ____
   ____
   ____
   ____
   ____

Gold Star Moments

1. _______________________
   ____
2. _______________________
   ____
3. _______________________

Vomit Bucket
Things That Still Needs Work

____
____
____
____
____
____
____
____
____
____
____
____

Things To Be Released

1. _______________________
   ____
2. _______________________
   ____
3. _______________________
   ____

REWARD:_______________________

If you're feeling grateful or generous, why not write a thank-you letter to the people who have always been there for you?

You don't have to share your letter, but writing it can be a therapeutic and healing experience. And it doesn't have to be perfect.

Dear ____________,

I just want to take a moment to say thank you. Thank you for being there for me when I needed you the most. You've always been my rock, and I couldn't have gotten through tough times without you. I hope you know how much I appreciate everything you've done for me.

With love,
[Your Name]

Do I have any outdated beliefs or values that are no longer serving me? If so, now is the time to let them go for my greatest and highest good.

Which ones can I let go of now?

Which ones do I need to work on before I can let them go?

What were my core values as a child?

Core Values List

Below is a list of core values. This list is not exhaustive, but it will give you an idea of some common core values (also called personal values). I recommend selecting less than five core values to focus on—if everything is a core value, then nothing is really a priority.

Authenticity	Kindness	Writing a yearly Core Checkup Report is a great way to help you hold yourself accountable for living out your daily values. So take some time each year and evaluate how you actually put these values into practice - it'll help keep you on the right track!
Achievement	Knowledge	
Adventure	Leadership	
Authority	Learning	
Autonomy	Love	
Balance	Loyalty	
Beauty	Meaningful Work	
Boldness	Openness	
Compassion	Optimism	
Challenge	Peace	
Citizenship	Pleasure	
Community	Poise	
Competency	Popularity	
Contribution	Recognition	
Creativity	Religion	
Curiosity	Reputation	
Determination	Respect	
Fairness	Responsibility	
Faith	Security	
Fame	Self-Respect	
Friendships	Service	
Fun	Spirituality	
Growth	Stability	
Happiness	Success	
Honesty	Status	
Humor	Trustworthiness	
Influence	Wealth	
Inner Harmony	Wisdom	
Justice		

How have my core values changed since childhood? Why?

Looking back at that list, what are my core values now as an adult?

____
____
____
____
____
____
____
____
____
____
____
____
____
____
____
____
____
____
____
____
____
____

List 7 things that make me proud of my past?

What did I not like about my childhood that I want to change in my adult life?

WHAT HAVE YOU DISCOVERED

LLL
Life Lessons Learned

1. _______________________________
   ____
2. _______________________________
   ____
3. _______________________________
   ____
   ____
   ____
   ____
   ____

Gold Star Moments

1. _______________________________
   ____
2. _______________________________
   ____
3. _______________________________

Vomit Bucket
Things That Still Needs Work

____
____
____
____
____
____
____
____
____
____
____
____
____
____

Things To Be Released

1. _______________________________
   ____
2. _______________________________
   ____
3. _______________________________
   ____

REWARD: _______________________________

Hello,
You're making great progress! Keep up the good work; you're almost there!

What lesson(s) from my childhood have stuck with me the most? Why?

Who do I think was responsible for the lessons I learned in childhood?

What is something that happened in my childhood that still bothers me today?

Why? What would it take to let that go?

What does my inner child need to hear?

Send a message to my inner child. What does it say?

Healing comes in waves, and maybe
today, the wave hits the rocks,
and that's ok,
that's ok, Boo

You are still healing.
You are still healing!
I stopped thinking of healing as a
destination,
embracing it for the journey it is, and
that in itself has been a healing
experience.

HOW ARE YOU COMMUNICATING?

HIGH REGARD FOR SELF

HIGH REGARD FOR OTHERS

ASSERTIVE
Remaining calm
Using "I" statements
Avoiding accusatory language
Standing up for yourself and
others in a positive way

AGGRESSIVE
Speaking loudly
Using "you" statements
Demanding in use of language
Interrupting others
Blaming others
Intimidating others

PASSIVE
Unable to effectively speak you
opinions and thoughts
Feeling walked over by others
Needs are not being met
Becoming resentful of others

PASSIVE AGGRESSIVE
Using sarcasm
Feelings and actions dont match up
Sabotaging or annoying others
Avoiding confrontation
Denying issues

LOW REGARD FOR OTHERS

LOW REGARD FOR SELF

MENTAL CLEANSE CHALLENGE

Set two goals you would like to achieve in this challenge

Go for a walk
Go to bed 30 minutes earlier than normal
Make a Gratitude List of all you are grateful for in your life
Take a long bubble bath
Try a new workout you have never done before
Keep all 3 meals "phone free" No social media scrolling!
Do a Yoga for beginners workout!
Meditate for 5 minutes & focus on your breath.
Take your workout outdoors, if only for 20 minutes
Clean out your inbox & sort your emails into folders.
No social media before 11 am! Take this time to be productive!
Unfollow people on social media who do not inspire you
Organize your desktop according to folders
Go through your phone and organize your apps
Have a phone-free night with family/loved ones
Unsubscribe from all unwanted email marketing
No complaint day!
Write down 3 great things that happened today
Spend 15 minutes in silence, focusing on yourself
Compliment a stranger
Write a letter to yourself explaining why you are unique.
Ask a couple of friends to describe you in 3 words
Write out your challenge wins & treat yourself!

RELEASE OF PAINFUL EMOTIONS

Become more open and accepting of the pain you feel.

The most common thing blocking people from releasing their pain is that they resist it.

Fully feel the pain so you can heal\True positivity isn't about ignoring pain or darkness, but opening our hearts to it and fully accepting it without wallowing in it.

Listen to the messages of your emotions and make necessary changes.

We often put ourselves in extreme conditions and get angry with ourselves for not thriving. As you tune in to receive guidance, make the changes you're guided to.

THIS IS ALSO TRAUMA

Being screamed at often
parents focusing on high achievements only
being reprimanded for making mistakes
being humiliated
being left alone often
being the one that takes care of siblings
working at a young age
moving to different houses/cities often
parent picking you up late all the time
parents comparing you to others
parents dismissing your emotions
parents picking a favorite child

We all have experienced traumatic events in our childhoods. It becomes trauma when we don't have anyone to defend us/support us/or protect us from these events happening again and again.

UNMET NEEDS

IF YOU FEEL:	YOUR UNMET NEEDS MAY BE:
Anxious	To have safety, security, and stability
Resentful	To feel heard, understood, and noticed
Numb	To feel supported, safe, and loved
Overwhelmed	To have space, support, and "me" time
Disconnected	To feel noticed, loved, and prioritized
Distrust	To have honesty, openness, and loyalty
Stressed	To prioritize yourself and self-care

YOU CANNOT MOVE ON

UNTIL YOU ACCEPT THAT...

You will not receive closure in every situation, but you can create it for yourself.
Most of what other people do is about them, not you.
Some things cannot be explained.
Some people won't apologize because they can't.
You cannot change people, no matter how much you think they need to change. People change themselves.

You may want to forgive your parents for the following:

Raising you through their own unresolved trauma
Not being able to teach you certain skills, as nobody taught them
Not being able to understand you because they did not have the
capacity to
Raising you through their own struggles, worries, pain, and fears
Doing the best they could with what they knew and had
Following certain cultural norms that they were surrounded with
Being emotionally unavailable, as their parents were emotionally
unavailable

Can you? Will You?
It's important to forgive as part of your healing process because it
allows you to let go of any anger, guilt, shame, or sadness you may be
feeling and move on. Once you identify what you're feeling, give voice to
it, and accept that mistakes are inevitable.

And please remember:
Forgiving someone isn't for their sake; it's for yours. You can release the
thoughts and feelings that have kept you tied to the past without the
other person's involvement. Forgiveness allows you to move on from
the regrets or resentments that take up your valuable energy and frees
your energy for something much more productive.

I now release what I don't want to make room for the desires of my heart.
I now forgive and release everything and everybody who needs forgiveness and release from the past or present.
I let loose you and let you go! I let go and let God do his perfect work in this experience for the highest of all concerned.

Release unwanted negative energy by writing down feelings of anger, guilt, frustration, or worries. Light a black candle to absorb all the negativity and burn the paper with the flame. Then light a white candle to increase positive energy.

I release all things from the past that have caused any negative attachments. I prepare and welcome new changes. new lessons and new adventures. I welcome new opportunities to grow emotionally. mentally and spiritually.

I rid myself and my space of negative energies. All negativity present be gone forever. I surround myself with white light, happiness, and positivity.

I give up freely give up what is no longer serving me. I release it to create space for what inspires me.

Today I have closed
the door
to the past...
opened the door to
the future,
and take a deep,
cleansing breath
as I step on through
to start the next
chapter
in my life...

NOW WHAT?

The whole point of these shadow work questions is for you to get to know yourself better. So by just writing down your unfiltered thoughts and reactions to them, you're already succeeding!

But what you do next with all of this information depends on your personal goal.

It's okay if some people prefer to keep their shadow work in their journals and only use it when they feel lost or overwhelmed. And that's okay.

Others like to dig deeper and implement changes (both big and small) into their lives based on what they discovered during their journaling sessions. Either way is okay. Remember, You do You!

If you decide to make the changes, you must analyze your answers to determine the underlying root cause or emotion.

Once that is done, you need to take that emotion and try to connect it with an experience, traumatic event, or time when that belief was challenged, which will be the next step in the healing process.

If you would like to continue this journey with me, then please continue on to the next book in this series, Titled Relationships. Yup, you guessed it. It is about your relationships past, present, and possibly future. Are you with me? I hope to see you there.

Blessings to You and Yours,
Robin Ginther-Venneri

Give yourself time to adjust

After you finish the shadow workbook, it is important to give yourself time to adjust. It can be a lot of information to take in all at once, and you might need time to process everything you have learned. Try not to put too much pressure on yourself and just take things one day at a time.

Read It Again

After finishing the Shadow Work Journal, one of the best things you can do is to reread it. This time, take your time and really reflect on each question and your answers. What did you learn about yourself? Are there any patterns that you see? Are there any areas that you want to work on further?

Seek out support

If you are struggling after finishing the shadow workbook, seek support from friends, family, or a professional. It can be helpful to talk to someone who can help you understand and work through the material. There are also many online resources and support groups that can be helpful.

Share Your Experience

Another great thing to do after finishing the journal is to share your experience with someone else. This could be a friend, family member, therapist, or anyone you feel comfortable talking with. Sharing your experience can help you process it further and give you some helpful feedback from someone else. Reading the journal together and discussing your answers can help to deepen your understanding of the material and can also be a bonding experience.

Use It as a Reference

The Shadow Work Journal can also be used as a reference tool in the future. For example, whenever you are in a situation where you're unsure how to proceed, you can refer to the journal for guidance. Additionally, if you ever struggle with negative emotions or self-doubt, you can use the journal to help you work through those issues.

Put what you've learned into practice

Once you have taken some time to adjust and process what you've learned, start putting it into practice in your everyday life. See how the shadow work principles can be applied in your relationships, career, and other areas of your life. Be patient with yourself, and remember that it takes time to change old thoughts and habits.

The goal of shadow work is to get to know yourself better. It can be used as therapy or as a tool for self-improvement, as long as you're honest with yourself. The important thing is to investigate which of your beliefs feel right and true to you. Only you can decide what changes (if any) to make based on what you discover. And remember that confidence and self-love don't come instantly—it's a process. So take the time to nurture this journey by accepting who you are today and continuing your self-love discovery tomorrow!

So don't be hesitant; take the plunge and continue your self-love discovery! It'll be a brave and fruitful journey that'll teach you so much more about who you are.

Remember, You Do You!

And as always, Blessings To You and Yours
Robin

I'm excited to announce that my next book in the self-help series based on shadow work and inner child healing is coming soon. So stay tuned for more information.

 Scan here for the latest release from Robin Ginther Venneri and KIPS Publishing

Thank you so much for your support!

If you enjoyed this book, then kindly leave a review on Amazon and on any of your social media accounts, and please tag me on them.

Thank You so much!
Blessings to You and Yours
Robin Ginther-Venneri

Questions, concerns, and ideas can be directed to
KIPSPublishingllc@gmail.com

How to Support Indie (Independent) Authors

Review their books
Like & comment on their posts
Share their in-story or about pages
Preorder their books. You know you are going to buy them anyway
Recommend them to other readers
Email or message about a book of theirs you loved
Follow them on social media

www.ingramcontent.com/pod-product-compliance
Lightning Source LLC
Chambersburg PA
CBHW060155120726
48004CB00007B/1548